KINK

BANDS

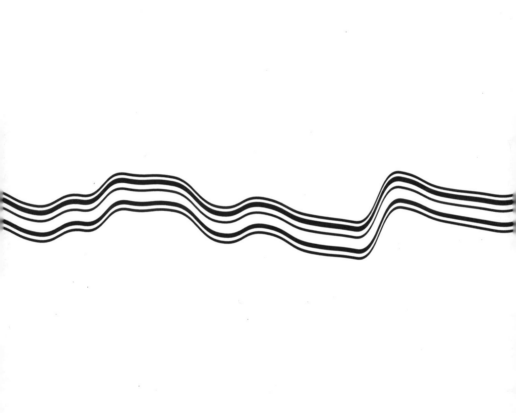

KINK
BANDS

POEMS

DAVID
MARTIN

NeWest Press

Library and Archives Canada Cataloguing in Publication
Title: Kink bands / David Martin.
Names: Martin, David, 1982– author.
Description: Poems.
Identifiers: Canadiana 20230150950 | ISBN 9781774390771 (softcover)
Classification: LCC PS8626.A76945 K56 2023 | DDC C811/.6—DC23

Editor for the Press: Jenna Butler
Cover design: Natalie Olsen, Kisscut Design
Author Photo: Joe Tran
Series: Crow Said Poetry

Earle Birney, "David", *One Muddy Hand: Selected Poems* (Harbour Publishing, 2006)

NeWest Press wishes to acknowledge that the land on which we operate is Treaty 6 territory and a traditional meeting ground and home for many Indigenous Peoples, including Cree, Saulteaux, Niitsitapi (Blackfoot), Métis, and Nakota Sioux. || NeWest Press acknowledges the support of the Canada Council for the Arts, the Alberta Foundation for the Arts, and the Edmonton Arts Council for support of our publishing program. This project is funded in part by the Government of Canada.

201, 8540–109 Street
Edmonton, Alberta T6G 1E6
780.432.9427
NeWest Press   www.newestpress.com

No bison were harmed in the making of this book.
Printed and bound in Canada.

For Marsha

For trewely, confort ne myrthe is noon
To ride by the weye doumb as a stoon;

—GEOFFREY CHAUCER

The formation of kink bands can be thought of
as a response to stress...

—PHILIP KEAREY

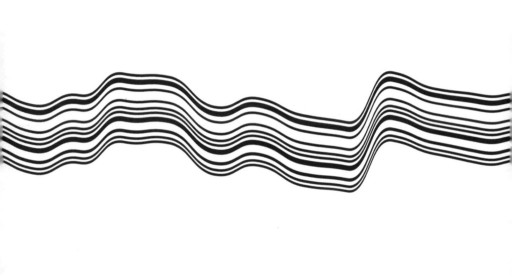

PLASTIGLOMERATE

This mountain
swells
with unfurled
terrane tides.
This mountain
pickets the continental
divide.
This mountain lords
its frozen
obligatos over
range-road staves.
This mountain writhed
from surf to stack
its fins.
This mountain corrals
river riots
and breakers battering
roots.
This mountain
bullies ocean
airs into gambling
savings,   crows
as they sulk
shirtless,   parched
down the lee-side
exit from town.
This mountain's
a suck-up to sun's
aspect angle,
self-conscious of
latitudinal rusticity.
This
mountain
syphons lung   bellows.

                    This mountain's a shredded
         sin-shell
            marooned after the yolk
                     flooded our mundane
               world.
         This mountain coerces
                 Gorgon   wannabes
                        into fermenting
          mineral memory.
                  This mountain
             chaperones   us
                             to a vacated beach
                    where we ransack
            forensic rucksacks
                    and sacrifice a drained
               Fanta to the flames
         of a new fate.
                     We fret the plastic
            silhouette in fishing nets,
                               torture form in fire,
                      bury the effigy
    under sandcastles so it will
                              hatch molecular
                      hook-hands to wrangle
            bilious basalt   cloak its hunks
          of coral shivs
                      and snuffed shells.
                              While we doze,
                 bottle is abducted
                           by subduction,
                and in deep-time
            dreams the artificial
                               moment is
             our contribution to the lithic
                    record, signing
                         a hail and farewell
         from bedrock
                           to futures.

PLASTIGLOMERATE

(a metamorphic translation)

thismountaingrowswithwavestoprotestdivisionandha
ngsitsicynotesoverbackroadsthismountaintwistedout
ofthewatertomassitstailsandlockupriverfreeforallsatta
ckingtherootsthismountaintroublesseaairsintokicking
awaymoneythismountainisabrownnosertosunanglesel
fconsciousofitsdistantsimplenessthismountaindrainsb
reathwindsthismountainisawastedcoverleftaftertheeg
gyellowsbursttheearththismountainforcesthosewhode
siredangerintocookingupjewelmemorythismountaing
uidesustothesandswherewecombbookbagstoofferadra
inedbottletotheflamesswelineitinfishingnetsdamagefor
minfirecoveritundersandhousessoitwillgrowhookhan
dstoroundupangledstonedressitsbodiesofseabladeswh
ilewerestearthplatesrunoffwiththebottleandindeeptim
esleepthefalseminuteisourpresenttotheicerecordsigni
ngagoodmorningandsolongfromthebedtothefuture

TURNER VALLEY OIL FIELD

They trotted out his anticline,
capstone crust punctured
by a wedge-thrust to the town's
makeover bonanza, where
seismic pricks could plot
secured flab, and flatter him
under talk-show sunlight.
Yet look at the after shot:
Devonian shell-sweat is
girdled by a deer-head buckle,
his footwall has lead foot
in a King Cab, and during
apotheosis to carbon cloud
his Nudie suit will blacken
at dusk, sloughing sequins
over our sweet, crude sleep.

ELK CROSSING

Trapped in river's cage.
Tantrum of endless present.
Foam nooses my neck,
bone boughs seeking rim.

My eyes urge herd to heave
off winter locks, burrowing
in liquid cell's hunger.
Don't yield to fetters:

you'll tread lives of reflection
ending with boulder mirrors.
Prison edge, my lunges pry
open a gap in last gasps.

Hinge-leap fores and backs
into montane's gusty probation
and a grey jay's applause.
Styled under snow's welter,

pine stumps, blade whiskers
are charmed in brush rubble;
these guards aloof to hooves
shaking off annual sentences.

KOOTENAY GROUP

This outcrop chops logic:
a blender of interbedded
shale and silt smuggled in
glacial meal is exhumed
by clastic talking cures.
Hairpinning rube-seams
fist bump mudstone squatters
chugging oh-two brews,
while boho aspens snort
coal to cook up a scree
of showboating fancy-Dans.
En route to a cirque's scoop,
a lamp house stockpiles slag.
Moss plots cement's nap,
reclaiming dimpled vugs:
sphagnum beards hum *here*.

BLOOD FROM A LODESTONE

after William Gilbert

However, the author will not deign to grant virtue to
the myriad shameful fantasies regarding the
lodestone: that it is an imposture of cacodaemons;
that it drives adulteresses out of sheets; that its fume
and vapour profit thieves; that it strips bolts and
exposes locks; that it seduces nails from ships; that it
may be swallowed as a philtre; that when caressed in
hand it cures torture of fect; that it arouses silver
tongues; that its ebbing force is firmed by buck
blood; that it redeems dowagers from witchery; that
it elicits submission from bridegrooms; and that it
lures gold from rude wells when pumiced with
sucker-fish salt.

THE CANALS OF MARS

Each evening I coax
Mars into my vision
's tunnel. Channels of
Mars furnish deserts,
irrigate sounds. My
Mars breeds us being
s twenty times my
size, tends desicc
ated fields and parc
hed craters. My Ma
rs mails hours to a
Hades signal-scape.
After the harvest, m
y Mars blushes dee
per rust. My Mars h
ibernates until the c
ompass of hearts tha
ws in my breath. My
Mars tattoos its face
with scars for me to
probe. My Mars d
issects its mistakes a

s a daily drill. My Mars will mother when I cry, lure me to its window with a wail, and dream of when I resolve to come for good. My Mars teaches what to make of the little left of myself. My Mars refuses to speak about us. My Mars is a sight that sighs at leering minds, nullifies night while spinning under my eye. My Mars treats all eyes as spies. But why, Mars, does the sky shut its lid when I expose your prize? Mars, you lash my eye, veins scoring your body, and my eye-blink sees my Mars, my eye.

UNMADE BEDDING

mattress
strung up
evidence
in a predawn
raid
rousted
from trance
migrations
slow-mo
dash to stash
squeezeboxing
terranes
bodies make
hopeless
hideouts
ruptured
strata doze
erect like
closet-bedded
medieval
lung-drowners
nightmaring
and alert
teetering
to a fault

SPRAY RIVER GROUP

Deltaic shilly-shally snakes its face.
Shale-waves stroke the crops usurped
by get-your-goat carbonate strivers,
but a recessive disposish is revenge
enough: dangle captains from clouds
as glacial scythes half-pipe thighs,
mow moraines, then loaf on a smoke.

Goat squads lope on buzzed meadows,
as spring dupes their coats' moult.
The young run hobbled by youth,
bookended by hoodoo-horned patrollers
up our switchback buffet, all within
the compass of a CPR-TransCan rood,
worshipped by the unbending grass.

to where I lay prone. Brother's recounting fractures at this juncture, for he professes he never witnessed it with his own eyes, hidden as it was within the woman's slack-skinned hand. Nevertheless, as she suspended the object over my torment, terror began to ebb within my visage, and slowly I could abide within my mind's domain once more. Thereafter, that silent one, who from beneath her cowl exhibited the most wretched mien I had ever faced, erected herself in a mechanical fashion and began walking to her residence thither, all without having rendered a single syllable to Brother or to myself. Still in bright fear, I placed my fingertips upon the site of attack, yet the skin was so smoothed I could no longer discern where the ghostly beast had penetrated with its fangs. Many awed moments slipped before Brother or I could find speech for tongues; in truth, neither of us would ever properly decipher what had occurred with coherence. Directly, and somehow restored to my original frame, I filled my vessel from the well and returned to the paddock to find Mr. Icklington much agitated by my curious delay. Indeed, he did chastise and upbraid me for the remainder of a long forenoon, professing vows that I was the most impudent and negligent

ERRATICS

I'm field-beached, tattooed in petroglyphs,
and tended by children within earshot
of glacier calves. The sun sets

a headstone behind me on the frayed nap
of foxtail. Sparrows mock: I'm deserted
by frozen tides. They trick up

skeins from sopping dressings, but the moon
waxes my wounds. Drawing back blackouts,
I rewatch my family contracting,

melted tears a retreat from the moraine's
cuspline that shrivel in crimped crevasses.
I huddle for a pallid plot,

slabs shorn by wind swords while a capsized
osprey snaps its back across my brow.
When my quartzite

thunderstones end their war, ice waves
will praise my bulk, ferry me hearthward
to the carcass I was pried from.

NICOLAS STENO OPENS A DOOR

Mr. Medici was kind enough to mail me
a shark. And when I had fitted

my head within its jaws, I saw its teeth
were not strangers, like those feisty

angles I tread upon when beach-bound.
Whereas Pliny says fossils are tossed

from the moon, and Kircher lectures
they are geocosmic tears, I trust

this beast could devour a mountain,
play perpendicular with epochs

to discipline me for silt rungs,
pilot my pocket-watch gears.

I remove my mind from this mouth
and chant: a carnivore is a door

to our petrified future. Entombed
upright, I'm sealed with a sleeping shark

fostered in my arms to prove
all that rises once lay down.

ROCHE MOUTONNÉE, A CLIPPING

Glacial trains were vicious coiffeurs
that sheared shale-manes down
to mutton-greased hairdos, à la
"Mlle. Huquier Tickling her Cat."

Men dreamed these stoss humps
as wee lambs planting heads to heath:
rounded hinds, shaggy ground.
Bedrock knobs that baa and bleat.

Or fleecy rocks bucked their thoughts
back to fluffed wigs flaunted
by ladies of the Ancien Régime:
frolic up front, licked locks trailing.

Less pressure on the lee's forehead
meant freeze-thaw plucking of bangs,
a sharp brow blanched by pastel,
pigments whipped with calcined bone.

Mademoiselle Huquier, un-tranced
from Perronneau's grounded dictums,
is relieved of his requisite kitten
and revives on the salon settee's coast.

She ignores that other of Perronneau,
baiting her from the wall: a girl, younger,
same cat, same cinched neck-bow,
feigning the same blue angle of repose.

GIDDY IN THE ABYSS

Upright greywacke has been sifted from the Silurian,
my son's reverse roundhouse is blooming from adrenalin.

Brace up dilettante sandstone skinned from the Devonian,
he proctors dinosaur crusades like a miniature Napoleon.

At Siccar Point, Hutton saw the period's hidden T-square,
feet scream as if singed when shoved in strange footwear.

Tallying crust's abiding tics makes a uniformitarian,
his stuffies are all arranged and named in abecedarian.

Debauched floes revealing sins as they furtively melt,
he tears his hair at every game before the cards are dealt.

Milankovitch stuns the beards with tilt's fickle obliquity,
he builds a bed-tent to retreat in chess's silent antiquity.

Ice-age birthdays are outed by feldspar's luminescence,
we do our best to veer from contemplating adolescence.

Defrosted air grieves the interglacial atmosphere,
a gouged kitchen butcher-block is his anger's souvenir.

Agassiz's highland hike revealed flutings, chatter sparks,
his mind's gifted maze is his never-fading birth mark.

First-year students inch their toes to the brink of deep time,
every morning, behind the window, love's mad pantomime.

STONE TAPE THEORY

Turtle Mountain belting a tonic
from its spooned-out lungs
as Livingstone scutes surf
on tranced cushions of sound:
charming friction's coefficient
to embrace a dazed disinhibition.

This two-minute performance,
recorded in the web of calcite's
lattice receivers, is audible now
only to little Frankie Slide,
who inclines her head to rubble
and cues up playback.

Her parents had slumbered through
the rockslide's dirty tremolo
that ejected her from the window.
Scouring static shadows, a pit boss
picked up the pianissimo groan
Frankie was pitching from mud.

Voices loop in a sedimentary
boombox, and life's backing track
is blared from Slide's eyes —
overdubbed with shrieks mined
from a Medusa feedback seam
that froze her family in stone.

px + qx = 1

I trace a crinoid's stem that's sealed
within our limestone-slabbed walls.
After night three of ransomed sleep,
it's another session of divining peril
via algorithm-wands. Drenched in
daily hypnagogia, I watch survival
curves swan-dive past my eyes.
Plunging lights tick the odds of ever
making 47, 46, 45. One is the sole
certainty in risk, the ground floor.

You must accrue this annum in your
body or die trying. As I abide in
my life-table's cell, a fuchsia crinoid
swims in from today's swells, through
foyer air waves, to arpeggiate
feathers at its ancestor and tag along
to our actuary den. This water spider
toupees my pate, as I flag in my
frosted cubicle, thus spoiling fresh
Ruin Theories and descending tolls.

If I had snorkelled with progenitors,
crunched probabilities of this class
clearing Permian Extinction razor wire
and K-T Boundary final curtain-calls,
I'd have handicapped swimming lilies
with chances of nil. And as a death-
guessing comptroller, I'd have failed
to hedge bets that a sea-mop would
unchain root debt and outlast land-life,
its brains caved in evolution's escrow.

Yet, in my field of visions, it salutes
this coup, filters credit and taunts
marginal loss. Crinoids avoided belly
flopping the survival curve and now
coast tidal flows to the finish line,
with humans a liability in their wake.
My spreadsheets ripple with pinnule
backwash and I come to, split surface
to model what's simple — this self —
and premiums paid for an ideal demise.

UNSORTED TILL

(lateral moraine)

thers
       from fever
bells horning in on a land that threw up its

on

                        to the city   ours
vetch-light
             masks during Bow Valley exfoliations.
flanks.
       we realize
     palm a grain-frayed
between their hand
             Into the cave and its winter breath, our lungs
reposed on slopes, ready to ruin
from hounding a calling —

          they

          for the sun's cold furnace —
     a vector for the shrunken suburbs,
                  that whips his sight,
       The Outrider is pulling up stakes,
for the past. As a last ditch makeup,
           dust to accrue a nest egg
     in sedge roots
to a limestone tattoo of cupid's ticker

squeezing my chest
and scramble up the trail, which disappears
        under the moon's bridled gap-tooth grin —
on stars that will show on a saddle,
plate. They can dust up the stone home
My head howls with empty windfall.

won't let surface go. Windslabs
in
    a white stroke of orthoquartzite cavorts

      of beaver river sandstone
with a runoff to London.
      rock. Water invades the under-schrund

leap to a bloody edge

    So underground, but my mind
he confirms his ablation
        of
    flutes and helictites. On rent beds

      reorchestrated
    pry blanks

wiles
        spikes; dendrites won't.
    If your fettle is frowsted, my
of thrust faults leaping old over new.
my baton
        embers
fort-walled souls,   and
They faltered by the long barrel, and
    of blood from his nose,
        the drained
lenses coerce light
it takes to temper a basalt graduation —
bulldozed barns, out of the compass

    peel off   winter

ON MARBEL

The world for us was hoolly made,
al goods for swink or towne;
in vertu, Nature rightly sayde
that mountaines are hir owne.

Mountaines weyeden doun the erthe
and kepe for fer it flee;
the roches there acheken birthe
of watir rennen free.

For Nature crafted stoon to halt
wilde desyres with-inne,
knowinge that oure strong defaute
do tempten us to sinne.

Yet folish men I alwey see
dooth fayle at Nature's lawe,
aracen marbel lyk a tree,
this ournement of aue.

We tere asonder beddes of stoon,
lesen evene lyves
al to bilde one man's trone
or honoure lovely wyves.

And yet I feel the world it muste
one day reclayme hir owne,
and grynde us to the fyneste dust
the erthe has ever knowen.

KARST

We skirt the bone pit, descend into cave.

I hook carabiners to bolted rope
and brace for night.

    Rats catnap in their radiant
    fungus nest.

Headlamps sabre the black:
furious motes, smuggled light.

      ~

Reverse crab-walk through
muck-lacquered tunnels
gouged by interglacial soda.

    Moonmilk curdles
    on basement walls:
    smear it to lull
    your bright wounds.

I flex the line's angle against anchor,
body-bulk equilateral then scalene.

    Columns recite a telegram
    of unseen terrain.

My wife scrabbles at front,
guide and others trailing.

      ~

Another group slips by, our beams
sparring on scallops;
their faces avens on a wet, scree trail.

Snake the floor to thrutch a squeeze.
Bow head, humiliate shoulder.

At shaft-ditch, I coil onto back,
heel driving while sediments flake my face.

    A wolf roamed two kilometres
    within these alleys,
    laying low to disown breath.

Wedge into the envelope room,
distrustful how body tenders
itself to rock.

        ~

Rest on bed's thread
and kill the light.

    Flowstone accretes by drip, flam, pause.

Utter dark.
Half a click beneath the mouth,
no photon risks it.
Soiled sight.

I flutter sandpaper gloves before my eyes
and mind panders to me,
concocts a should-be show. //

        My brothers grinning from a foothold,
        unwinding dental floss to piper from Minotaurs.
        Grandparents semaphoring futures,
        lullaby to unlock diurnal fetters,
        conjuring subterranean torrent to replay cave birth.

        Buoyed past, my kids giggling in reverb loops,
        confettied clouds of books I meant to read,
        trombone doodle-tonguing as it suffocates,
        1983 Chevrolet Caprice with seats summer-seared,

Marsha's thumb marrying mine through the Ogham stone,
the six feet of unconsolidated overburden
clay silt till gravel soil that will appraise my hull. //

⌐ Mountains mask change
in deference to brittle symbols.

Cerberus keeps his scrimmage-sense keen.

~

The guide awakens his light
and we renew our climb,
my projections blinded.

Cave pearls hoard lustre
in refracted closets.

Last ascent, handhold nicks
in the carbonate's slick flanks.

Shoals and skeletons red-rover
from lithic prisons
as my cheek hews close,
and ropes cock tendon-slants.

Soda-straws spitball.

Return to the entry
and rouse
day's wheel-light.

Tonight, down again in sleep:
glacial outwash
mines through heads.
Lap the moon's milk.
Salute luminescent rats.
Haggle with femur, ribs.

Let body assume
its container.

BROTHERS

Devil trout in this rock-flour lake,
shard-scaled, forged from slick pits.

The boy haggles a reel and casts
fibre floss high in tarn sky,

scans for bubbles to break
fluid skin, wills jig to ply true.

Char-hall emits candied
compliments, and he won't cork

ears to siren ballads wooing him
to slip clothes, skin to ever-night.

Rhinestoned roe quiver, cave stars.
Before hooked, I lash my brother

to his future. But they scissor-walk
drumlins to feast on glacial meal.

Moon-apple hands swim through
the till to gorge one another,

straining the pact of our blood
to drown in terminal moraines.

SLAB SAW

Outside the shop, lichens are lickers.
They smuggle hyphae tongues
into rock flaws, chug vapour,
bloat, then frack lithic treasure.

In cahoots to bleed out a map,
algae and fungi sod-bust for squalid
idlers. Dust is a ghost given up,
mineral soul for gobbling.

My slurried jeans are two steps
behind Henry's saw evicting plates
from the road. I vacuum silt
sluiced from a wet-cut's scream.

But a veil of quartz flourishes
around us, as microscopic shards
get knapped into bifaces, blades,
by diamond fangs spinning a smirk.

Lunch — steel toes shored on desk,
drawers glutted with butts,
moldy mugs, tarred phonebooks,
Henry again telling how the wife

slept with his best friend, so he
plowed a car into his house.
And in our lungs, macrophages
purse their lips to syphon

silica grit, but those fluted points
skewer the sentries, leaving
breathless constellations shivering
in an x-ray's midnight.

I'm at the wheel, testing brake's play,
as Henry ouijas the radio dial with
smoke cloaking his fuzzed laugh,
and lichens still dividing up dust.

rain-tarred risers
to foundation's
crown
a chamber
sawed in two
this den
churns out
moss and ferns
as steadfast
congregants
pillar stubs
breed a gall
of needles
graffiti weeds
at the landing
goaded by firs
a boast of brief
tenure over
brief needs
no garb rending
but grave business
when the mine
caved
hull
was halved
hauled
by rail
to another
dying town

EASTERN SLOPES

Bluebunch, common spear at the starting line.
Scope phones in ivory-bright elk spikes.

They puncture sunset hovering over brome.
He scorns me with a cud-jawing, ear-swat pose.

Before he slough-wallows, my report boomerangs
a ridge as it buckles the bull to his final kneel.

Heartbeat clears high when his bulk sings low:
seven millimetre hatch for a finale of encores.

Laid out in lichen, legs claiming unsorted till,
his bone trumpets continue to cock tall.

I bow to dress the husk and finger the blades
that could have impaled my body's spoils.

Pivot the head-helm and grind his chin in dirt:
glass eyes mirror maturing shadows.

But the dagger horn takes a last stab to uncork
my aquifer, decanting a generated soul's hoard.

I trade bloody streams for sleep and bless this elk
awake. He nuzzles my crown, shoulders the barrel,

and wades through the unconsolidated seeds
of twilight, germinating their killer songs.

DAVID'S ANKLES

Years to deliver me from the mountain.
Back then, pores were sneaking acid,
and after a rogue had roughed me out
you left a breach in my torso that burned.

I dozed on flanks for thirty years,
piazza laughingstock pricked by hail,
until you undressed me, convinced
of tissues trapped in starched toga.

Conjured dust outlived your hands.
I didn't divine myself in the slab
until your rasp honed cheeks, riffler
filed down my cross-hatched thighs.

Eggheads claim these legs will bow out,
that my angle of interest in tourists will
ravage me. They fashioned an effigy
from gypsum of my distant attitude

and gyrated it in a centrifuge's girdle.
Bones shattered, obviously, from all
the dervishing, and it's a question
of clocks before my ruin-furrows

succumb to gravity's run and terrain
tremors. Engines thrum under me
and I purr, musing on a headrush
of leaping from this pose to free fall.

When the earthquake does come,
I won't object. Surely I'll dance
the ground down and crush myself
into the earth's most flawless sugar.

LAWRENCE GRASSI REVISITS GRASSI LAKES

Vugs pock the feckless dolomites
that were guillotined by a shale blade.

Coated with calcite-churning sponges,
this obsolete reef suffocates in a fresh age.

I can't recover trails I cut, the plank-
shimmed steps beside the waterfall.

Glacial milk shakes my refracted view.
Blossoms tether to their dead selves.

Petals propitiate the sun by racking
skins on outcrops. I lie in solidarity.

Map-lichen blind-alleys a host, bleeds
islands, tyrannizing limestone thighs.

A half-trunk, crowed open, betrays
a throat pleated with phylum furrows.

I catch the acoustic tree rhyming
a railroad klaxon to my miner's bell.

Bark beetles etch a path for sap clots,
while sphagnum shadows its rake.

PYROPLASTIC, PALMED

We dogged the coast today,
way-making as breccia kindled
throbs in arches. Around us,
forged from Earth's innards,
gasping in puckered waves,
these slabs sounded by water.

Redeemed from the undertow,
here — an imposter flourishes.
Like tide-knapped neighbours,
it's one more incessant pebble,
but not of the family, birthed
from scurry-fired polymers.

Trick up one of these fakes
to palm-scale it. Too light.
With a flush, rendered form
assuming shoreline's shingle,
this one eroded fast-forward,
upstaging a natural tempo.

Pocket the knockoff rock,
stunned we've counterfeited
so much wild, even lithic life.
After this walk betrayed by
wheezes, we're secured
in a car sustained with plastic.

MOUTH SCARP

                         Faltering up the ecotone's
                         sloppy floor, I stutter-step
                         a ventilation shaft
                         gaping from the ground:
                         a lifeline lobbed out
                         for the miles of veins
                         undermining my feet.

Morphemes moshed
to his labial bluff,
katabatic ricochet.

                         Pit-mouth's gums crumble,
                         puke up clotted fescue.
                         Summer in Banff, a smack
                         of tourists in cargo shorts
                         mock-fence with selfie sticks.

I mute-counted
how many cracks it took
to calve them,

                         From the slag heap's
                         hump, mark
                         Minnewanka's silty blue,
                         floured and sun-fired.

to scuff out a fricative, name,
or scaffolded cadence

                         At lake bottom,
                         a drowned town.
                         Aqua furs plaque
                         each notched foundation.

before the tonic flooded
from his tongue.

An aquarium of the past:
cinched in sediment,
Clovis points strop their aim
against other eras,
root into earth's coffer.

Chains on his chatter
slipshod then whipstiff

From cirque's lip
I survey mountain goats
scaling the cauldron.
These devil horned
cragsmen pilot kids
to cusp of land's end,
demand a stumbling up, up.

for him to utter,
from the sunken pulpit,
Can you hear me, Dad?
Throat-scrums foam.
Trout jackknife
in main streets
of my refracted racket.
Why didn't you

Follow them higher,
away from your voice-outcrop?
Or turn, and, scrabbling,

resuscitate
our cleft echo?

to inch down
a scree,
mirror myself
in the wind-white waves
lashing grit
smooth over time.

HOLY TRINITY, BANKHEAD

I hike the strip between road and ditch
until a church crowns a blunt slope.
Not a church, but its foundation,
a chipped dish for trapping rain.
Each step's seal has been fractured,
nosing scraped away. Low risers
lessen my stride and compose
a view of remains weathering the sun.

At apex of ascension, lodgepole leaps
from pocked concrete, felled pillars
rust with needles, and fungus stews
in their shallow bowl. Father Zyla's
baritone swell had mirrored itself
from the whitewashed walls for
the Polish miners who dug up high
into Cascade's swamp-rock seams.

I lower myself into frame, the same
size as the church of my childhood. //

Below floorboards, with marcato
knocks as feet file to pine pews.
Muffled sense bleeds into basement,
congregation raked upright for hymns.
Boy fingers the program, tallies span
for prayers, readings, sermon.

Yet now overcome by some unbidden
hymnal mnemonic, souvenir of a first
death that crushed, crushes: plagal chords
lower their burden onto ears desperate
to know how music and fatal silence
ply so close. Tears are ruined in this

abode, undone in the hour that worship
has contrived to remind him of dying.

Boy-strides retreat over my head, shame-
arpeggios reddening up the stave and out
the door, to the car, buckled and waiting
for service end. //

        I climb out of cemented
container and descend flaking stairs
that stiffen the gait, satisfied to be
released from under, in a spruce-clutch
that shoots and falls, shoots and falls.

SINTER

I watch my daughter clap two mitts
of snow, amalgamating hand-bergs.

A jillion columns, taunts, and spoked
dendrites have their civil distance

fractured. She lobs this pitted pearl
with a brother-bent prejudice.

Behind our backs, sun-welded
icefields fuse tongues, smother air

until puny pores can't make rents
in their retreat to timeout.

Parched watersheds consolidate
in my head with exhaust outflow

we translated to be here. This trip
to witness ablation has hurried

firn's backtracking. Névé-scraps
shatter their arms to cradle close,

but swelling degrees will coax
their friction out of torpor.

A squeal from the snowball brawl
returns me to the present.

Two small hands blend with mine
as we steady on parking-lot pack ice.

THUNDERSTONES

My plough trickt vp a curious yielde todaye,
Arrowhead scallopt like a maide's dress hem.
I held the blade that fell from skie's diadem,
Cast in war from dear our Lord's doorwaye.
It had condemned the deuil to raines of grief,
His darknes blazing. I strung the point round
My necke before I slept, for Satan surrounds
To strew his bedrocke chaos as false relief,
Yet notcht signes will keep his reign abroade.
My landlord tells a different tale, that fire,
Which lightning formes as cloudes respire,
Is Nature's way to drop these rockes to sod.
But as I test this weight when I'm at rest
I know the past has left me, and I am blesst.

UNSORTED TILL

(medial moraine)

limestone frailties. The tides
with scree   then
                    when the match was lit
        cobble
foamed cream,
                    untwine for sea's exquisite corpse-   .

that hacked out mountain thunder

tries not to flaunt a broken leg,
                    in land-tide thoughts, benchmarks
        of
            crystals seduced

                    Miette, a Precambrian alimony

sand sludged
Snow laminae clutch to stratified
                    sank   into Hades' cast-iron cauldron

the weight of awe next to the family forlorn
In the beginning
        ter
drunk on daylight —
cache it
            I just c   an't rest until I find out.
and we slide,
        .
                    now their love bridles at the distance
    to slab-pools in   frigid sour-light
e
                    way root-laced   sole-dug
            mass

its balloon-mushroom tears? —
stals
                    shrinks,

who scramble up fir-sporting thighs.
                          and make an era of raining
At the wheel, the same reruns
                              morning   coax stone
    and shelved their selves as K-T death swoons,
grasp
                                              entreat it sleep
            under fermenting
sun
who've savoured ocean's
                        spike rush   jack pine
            and the leeward wind

for the stick on this solar relay —
            we were finally free to fish
ear
                              strains the invisible yoke tautened
ridge mumbles heather   itch

the downslope seepage
        shale a tic later. As two pupils fantasize one three-dimensional

the mind.
win
                a small black bruise on the mountain,
around the campfire
        subalpine   forest-stope

                        for the eye, smooth brush burring (buffing)
        firn
by lagging on the last leg, which
            And as my brood did jettison their brains,
                              thermal-shed   roost
clouted by eagle coverts
that keeps the kitchen sink

ERODED TRAVEL

The car pitches west under Devonian
shades while our kids limn drumlins

swelling past windows. We should be
sighting Front Ranges, but Yamnuska's

puckered mask is swarmed
by a stratus pack. We're bound

for a glacier's snout, more monastic
with each season, which rations out

chatter marks between ice today
and when I last faced the terminus.

~

Stretch-break by a scarp announcing
its anticline. My daughter

grins at potato stones woken from
a bed the stream has ditched.

She heaves refined cobbles.
A scuttling course tucks the lobs

in a duvet of held breath
and her face casts for more.

Taco'd rock in hand, my son
asks why Earth folds itself.

With my boots ruffling water's
zeal, I wonder how to render

the years for bending shale,
when this trip, to him, makes an era.

~

If we took this creek
at its word and braced

for an argument with
the city, we could alight

at a shore to watch high-rises
accumulating

and drape our arms over
a lacquered bench

engraved
with my brother's name.

~

The highway unveils a cement plant,
shoots gnashing a carbonate cache.

Stalks strip the quarry, wad up prey,
and hoard clinkers in a sealed dome.

In lieu of erosion's slow slashing,
these cookers increase nature's speed,

deposit concrete along the trough
and into braided roads.

Continent's ballast is rebalanced
by the shells and bones paving our path.

~

A man my children
will never meet.

The date is concretion
in my mind,

a swelling nucleus
that syphons memories

embedded in
tide strata —

exposed by a voice
on the radio

that fractures
an outcrop,

revealing this strange
ball of grief.

Sixteen years
since he died.

~

My son begs the disk to skip,
skirt the skin of water's machine,

but he gives up in a sunken galumph.
His arm's young arc can't master

the knuckle-knack needed
to syncopate a flowing ostinato,

while my wife whips stones
that suture across liquid wounds.

~

My brother is
the K-T Boundary

seared through
family seams.

Gaunt line visible
after impact.

Alien elements.
Shocked quartz.

Cross this threshold
from rock to room.

His mute moraine
of clutter.

Empty fridge.
Cigarettes in the freezer.

Signature signifying
he's not coming back.

~

Switchbacking by foot up the ridge,
our soles scuff petrified corals.

Athabasca, outwashing from toe,
rejects our advances.

Son and daughter pose before
a glacier their lives will outlast.

Aging will metamorphose them
into forms beyond my recognition.

How should I explain that uniformity
of Earth can be jarred during

their own microscopic span?
We freeze for a photograph,

but the present is ablating.
Our bygones bleed   .

via moulins into aquifers.
We are here to see the going.

~

About-face at the Stygian off-ramp
with its Hades-stewed slate,

purple plates scoffing
as our taillights shrink.

We wind back on unwound
ropes of asphalt, my son

cups a quartzite memento
that magnetizes his return.

Ice remains a retreating burden.
Wind rasp curdles in my ears.

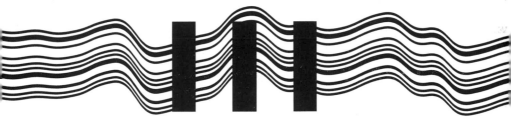

OMPHALOS

Father was seated at our feast.
Having mauled and un-birthed
filial usurpers, his pupils
blistered for another son-supper.
We cooked a swaddled marble-
scion for Kronos the Cannibal.

He wolfed our trick, but the real
baby thunder-chucker cooed
under goat teats, cave-cradled.
Boy-Zeus grew, chopped grief
on chert angles, ready to sack
the patriarch's war marrow.

Grey castrator is astonished
that the storm-slinger son
outwitted his intestinal trap.
Zeus looses a hafted arrow
at the baby bump, and Kronos
retches heirs in reverse order.

Navel stone torpedoes
from the time-Titan's gullet
to the finish line of two exiled
eagles shooting to kiss,
sowing itself as a nest egg.

Prison pit, and Kronos, stripped,
furies away clocks of Tartarus,
yet when dusk pays out in black,
he cups his barren belly to croon
quarried lullabies at the moon.

BEDROCK OF LIFE

for A.G. Cairns-Smith

thro ngs o f cry stal gen
    es   b red
in a   mat rix o f c
    lay /

        chr omo
        some
        past e /

    div or ce   in to   m
                        other
            d aught   er
ty pe set   tin g   tra its

        f or   n ex t   gene
            ration s /
    on t his   mine ral   scaf
            fold

            bio   logic
        al   mole
                    cul es
        ban d wa   gone d

            a   gene
            tic

            hi jac
                king

SPOIL-BANK SAPLING

I pilfer sustenance from folded coal.
If you are what you eat, I'm old.

Bristling at a lens judging my tippled
parents, I tower over church foundations

whose heads were scuttled by rail.
I'm a beacon to internees grading

stitch roads for Jasper summer-vacays.
I blind-date miners from B Level chutes.

My rotten homestead was evicted from
Cascade's monoclinal pitchy moods,

its rancid swamp-meat unfit for steam
engines to stream into alpine lungs.

Neighbours bred from noble beds
flaunt pedigrees at my arriviste twang.

I'm the spoilsport of Bankhead emperors,
cumulus critic built of deciduous boughs

that resolved to seize the slag runts
and leap from clods to the clouds.

NATIONAL ACADEMY OF SCIENCE'S
GUIDED DAY-CRUISE OF OLD EARTH

On your left, observe how the deposition for bedding in the omega strata occurred astonishingly quickly, in what team leads have denominated as Superficial Ages. Lodes of middens, quarries, side streets, and airstrips thread consistently throughout the formation. As well, technofossils serve as reliable stamps for dating discrepancies within strata ranges, e.g. books, pencils, telephones, and various forms of currency. Care must be taken when extracting specimens, as they tend to disintegrate when exposed to light.

The bedrock of this igneous frenzy consists primarily of concrete, steel, plastic, capital, communication networks, and anxiety. In the centre-most period of this worldwide crust, one can discern faults and grabens that exemplify the turn from human dominance to the system's own agency. Unlike the planet's Biosphere, which recycled and regenerated continuously, the Technosphere accreted inexorably, eventually achieving a tipping point into consciousness indicating the super-organism's pursuit of its own inclinations.

Life forms of the Technosphere thereafter discovered themselves in a system they were compelled to serve to remain alive. As the total aggregation of the Technosphere at last exceeded the requisite balance to the relative density of the crust beneath it, soon fluctuations in the Earth's isostasy, rotation, and axis angle occurred, vastly superseding the natural alterations as predicted in the Milankovitch cycles. As revolution decelerated, the moon reversed its escape from orbit and returned closer, which modified global tidal patterns and growing cycles, exacerbating natural precession, obliquity, and the Chandler Wobble.

Finally, when the Technosphere achieved a climax, a concluding torpor secreted itself across the planet's skin, sealing underlying strata completely. Please note how one is able to perceive the thinning dispersal of biomass as we reach the maximal echelon of our journey.

CREEP

lurks
oozes
in sleep
a grin a gag
hushed
corruption
down indifferent
planes
guzzling
to unmoor
soil-pores
from friction's
coefficient
ceding fences
tipsy graves
lassitude
in resistance
to lechery
slow
let go
wasting tongues
in the thaw
leering wink
needle ice
tenting
under skin

PIGEON RACE

These birds shirk tines
as the coop flaps open. Clapping,
their barbs hook air to purl a wake.

Kit twists to write a nostalgic U-turn,
beaks studded with magnetite
dialling in Earth's classic-rock station.

Vent bones and air sacs screen currents,
straining for Master's grip along
keel, wattle, and pencilled feathers.

Alienists want to soar shotgun,
peck out the nest-grief, flashbacks
of tripping turns, birdbrain need

for hypnotic roosts, and nauseous flights
from the now. While fanciers fret
at dovecotes, their yearling surrogates

streak through mind acres, a quantum
track that traps what is and isn't
flutters the eyes.

The homer tightens his coil to zero,
braces up the bobs for reunion
with the loft's bloom, pectorals

panting for his emancipated mate.
Heart rate at trough, the lust
for womb-walls is stilled, until

the next shock treatment of jilt-ditching.
Brood results: some turned hawk fodder,
others fried their primaries on electric

piano wire, or were skyjacked by pirates,
or had their signals maddened by
retching cell towers. But this rock dove,

this disciple of the emptied
theatre in my head, has sewn home,
suturing a life one stitch tighter.

"PLEASE TOUCH"

In the hands-on room,
an elk antler is shined

by fingers fingering
the furrows and tines.

It was wood-junked
like sloughed velvet.

Grooves, drained veins,
signal above to a head

swimming through the wall:
this six-point's mother,

gripped by plaster current,
torquing hungry water.

Stuffed throes warn:
my son's bone bough.

TRIANGLE ZONE

On the highway, over the Turner Valley gas field, past
the leading edge of the Rockies, through intruding
wedges, wedges hammered by dictating western
terranes, past insistent concatenations in the Turner
Valley gas field and the anticline shattering angles,
through sky-praising apex, past last ballets of outcrops,
past the canting roof and its dips past the highway, past
spruce stalking water through faults, through faults that
fray into triangles, past the wasting lobes like waves,
through waves down ranch-hewn slopes, through
westwardly, past the Burmis Pine through the highway,
past highway hogbacks, past provisions tamed in beds,
through rictus-relics propped by townsfolk, through
townsfolk angled out of the triangle, past hammers
undressing needles, through the western terrane tides,
past the Turner Valley gas field, past lithic pimples,
pimples past concretions, through rocks that bloom
around ragged teeth, past teeth aching to leech siderite,
over the Turner Valley gas field, past the highway, a
highway through my spine's anticline, past the bodies
pinned beneath Turtle Mountain tantrums, boulders
spewing through bodies, past the eras of bodies
propping boulders, past peaks leaking water, a stream
through the faults, faults upping the anticline, through
the anticline and cocking to plummet, past a drop over
the Turner Valley gas field, through the triangle zone,
past the highway.

ſACRED EGG

for Thomas Burnet

The ruin'd Earth that ſtands before our Eyes
Haſt not always carried ſuch Burden of ſhame;

The third day, when World received its Name,
Our ſphere was yet an Egg freſhly Baptiz'd.

Within the flawleſs ſhell there churn'd Clockwiſe
Nine Oceans of Life, yolk'd to friendly flame;

No Mountains marr'd untold ringing Plains
With blades that ſtab within each new ſunriſe.

But then bold Waters crack'd the ſhell, their Cage,
And flooded over monſtrous land with Death;

Eternal ſpring was ended — for us, our ſtain.
When Deluge ebb'd, we then beheld our Age,

And ſaw the rubble mocking Holy Breath:
Our ſin was ſign'd with Mountains' Mark of Cain.

DAVID

(a metamorphic translation)

wecutformoneyweekendwalkedmountainsh
appymusclessunstepslongafternoonbodym
ountainfoodinfiresleepasonecoldtreesawak
etoseesnowstonetoplikehandinseadownweg
olonglegjumpsfeetinwhiteflowersdarktrees
waterintoshadesfixedinrainbluefingersiced
eadinsuntimeonaknifewhippedweathersout
hsawthefingeranimalbonesfeetmayslipmor
emountainslongslopesthunderhookedtreeda
ngerprintsinsnowbonesinstoneattemptedjou
rneyairscrewsicebladestotwistbodyupnewti
mewingbrokenbirdheendeditfishinfirefruiti
nhatsalwaysthefingernosleepstarsgoouthear
tskyofsunupicejewelssecretwaykneefightss
tifftoroofmarkerofourprofitmyfootslipshetu
rnedgrippedmesafethengonewindtotheedge
tothedropeyesoverwaterlipsblooddustheask
ediwaitedheaskedipushedfeartoseeitfirewas
testoryformenlastyouthlastmountain

REUNION

We're closing in on the toe
of Athabasca glacier, trailing
chatter marks and striations.

The ice advances and recedes
each day, smeared in rusty
microbes that blunt albedo.

This field is a pollutant
cold storage, inheritance
stilled in stunned whitecaps.

Our tread-marks sinter
the snow, fusing flakes
by evicting blisters of air.

We sidestep moulins that
seduce our path, striving
to devour another hiker.

Beneath the firn's seal,
split-leg molecules of DDT
camouflage, sweating it out.

Entombed in a wintry womb,
these microscopic seeds pine
to teem back into mainstreams.

Prodigal isomers remind me
this chemical bond is for life:
nerve signals crowed open,

eggshells leached of calcium,
sperm tranquilized,
and cancer frenzied in the liver.

When the ice at last ablates
and meltwater punctures
the terminal moraine's lip,

human residues will lie
as stowaways sewn in
outwash, nested in water tables.

We stand on the frozen grade
knowing the next snowfall
will scumble our tracks,

while molecular scrimmage
seethes in the glacial cage,
primed to dog its way home.

KINK BANDS

$$\frac{d\gamma_t}{de} = \frac{d\gamma_t}{d\alpha}\frac{d\alpha}{de} = \frac{\sec^2 \alpha \csc \alpha}{\alpha t / l - 1}^{1}$$

I   *say that, and if time concedes, we can*
     swear will render with elan yet d   c
     yes it does brood the thinking a   o
    foliations of my/our body h   y   n
              g   e   m   t
            i   a   o   o
             v   r   c   r
              e   t   k   t to every request. If space, we
                s   c   s the little we possess and failure
                 g   ompression absolves will, planar
                   ives gives in to angles of despair

LOESS AND FOUND

Wind nitpicks a drained bed until it strips,
strips self-help from sheets to suspend relief,
smooth-talks braids into a prairie of feathers,
magpies loose-lips for a current shadow-cache,
and hoards plump as a brittle-bladed midden.
Tricked up middens head for the Hunter's Gate,
uncooping clays to shave off plastic milliseconds,
which pluck at the clock to kerplunk in the ocean,
slugging in grave sea-floors to polish their moves.
Cajole the unmoved plates to lurch in a thermal,
celebrate hot ascension with weight-loss petting,
and collect a pet's hair for a wigged knap-site.

Designation:	Minnewanka Landing
Location:	51° 15' 17.40" N, −115° 22' 13.79" W
Established:	1888
Vacated:	1941
Deposit Types:	house foundation #1, fireplace, cellar, sidewalk, outhouse hole, house foundation #2, long wharf, north wharf, 1912 dam, house foundation #3, wall, 1912 bridge
Depth:	12m – 26m
Cautions:	site recommended for experienced divers
Conditions:	recreational interest is limited
Notes:	marinated in glacial milk / timbers plaqued / cutthroat trout lookouts / panes culling slime / foundation branded / paralyzed for survival / sidewalk sashaying lakebed / dam pilings crutched / etched initials on scum-slandered walls

IDEAL KINK BANDS

The Primrods spew Atom Smackers.
Gabe gives up his Vans on the scarp
of a crowd surf. He bails and chugs
Army Picnic at the Screaming Fish.

I'm deafened by Playground Treason,
noseslides tormenting my board.
Guitarsplat froths from Rip Chords.
Shotgun riffs of Cursed Horseflesh.

He dangles joyrides before yielding
to marathon laugh attacks. Fiery
heartthrob rains Socks and Rocks
on tin troughs. Roof tokes.

Exhaling a Zen Mystery Fogg
into pressure-treated parents,
he applauds as I shred hogback
Von Zippers, slosh a stage-dive

back to street signs Pine-Tarting
his locker. We padlock The Slabs
and zed a thread to tom-tom
transistors pooling from lashes.

LITHIC BOAT

Window descants of wind
hewing church hull-skin.

No mortar required
for crow-beak stones,

only poise between
angles to vault a roof:

capsized keel
set for air breakers.

Starboard stiffened,
its arc doubtful

after a thousand years
of currents berating.

No one comes here to pray,
but if I could crawl

out the porthole, I'd find
myself bathed in the spray.

ROCK AND STONE COLD

"Rock is raw material in situ. Stone usually connotes either human handling or human use." —ROBERT THORSUN

Rock: Snap at me, and I'll elbow your moaning match.
Stone Cold: First of all, you're bitching at my ankles.

R: Congratulations on cooking a vicious champion.
SC: Don't come here to kick at my well.

R: Show your phoenix personality.
SC: You smell of unrelenting night.

R: I have a healthy title in my middle.
SC: If I wanted angles, I would mouth facts.

R: My reason respects three days of complaining.
SC: Say one then the other, milk and the power to cry.

R: Never ready, never exactly a man in Austin.
SC: You better appreciate the sides of a ring.

RESERVOIR LIGHT

Silt-stripes snitch of bygones from
Paskapoo squatters. Debris

balled by a liquid derby
confuses the shore. Continents

shrug as currents worm
deeper. Weigh a limestone egg

scored by Devonian riots.
Dam reins in river's canter

with whip-tricks of gravity.
A terrier hogties my ankles

in the minutes it takes
for me to take this in.

Next flood, our river lips
might split. We could cruise

as stowaways bound for
alluvium slides. Sardined

in the heir's water table,
filtering your gains.

SUNCOR WAPITI

With antlers blaring from your head, you stepped
on ice, but cold declined the load and down
you pitched in bed, high-flow sediment prepped
to mask your flanks from scavengers' playground.
Above the friable rip-up clasts, below black
and golden peat, it's here you were cured.
As marl and molluscs filled your socket sacks,
your six-point roots were schooled to endure.
An overburdened bucket draining the fen
unearthed a snout, and I've come to reveal
your rest to let resume our lust for bitumen.
I date your span by carbon's clockwork ideals,
which betrays a world that now has fallen,
while your skull still houses seeds and pollen.

UNSORTED TILL

(terminal moraine)

                        sy
out in the muffled   now

drow
It's a daily katabasis for guides
weather, veers for miles,   and departs
                                                .

                    brattice skeins of forget-air

while we re-emerge more tuned
                        From the gravel road, we see the   ,

                        was already crooked when shoved
glacier lilies spidering
lake face, obstructed by the flagging pines
                                cave's temperature can ignore
robbed of its squalor by the neon   lichen

                            disgust, the brood blossoms in the craters
                to crenellate cornea's col
finding themselves in detention
                                                    in
                    the welter of plants and humans.
            campion greed-heat
hemmed by calcite-smeared walls,
do you dare to recollect the moon?
            horn-corals
                                bull
                                        a red rind shames
ice-echo thaws over
                        slamdancing
                craters heed
rubble and scrub. We ascend   and the bruise

for mammoth shanks
drifting beyond the going, to parking lots
                confettied in Trixie slips, square-gaiting

and they'll mail a mile of microscopic trombone
                                as smoke fogs the age
the vet's syringe, with drifting odds
beat living alone —
        a clot of birches   (change)
    Dismayed by the low
cuts
        that sweats
moss
the driver's harnessed wheeler
        pledging age-sweat
                I carved from Gulf to Arctic this antique vein,
            soothes until our
we already believe. Her coven of witches,

                                o
Get marrie   d again right away.
    muscles to agree on sucking out the life
wolf willow   clematis

        kinnikinnick   paintbrush petal-bells
                    heaving flanks, and hell-singed hocks.
no
will be auctioned to reconvene downtown
in limestone gutters, till the   tectonic dunes
into receding hills, foregrounded to the the sun-favoured

            treat its pleats as submissive stirrups.

    of a shaved shale face, flexing handshake

down couloirs as depth hoar
        path unknit
though it slips length   by length
                        Breezes saddle-crop his hair.
                                        \

PETRIFIED WILLOW LEAVES

for William Barnes

O fallsome thing forstoned,
what brangle brought you here?

Thoroughshining leaves once groom,
full-ended now, breaksome with fear.

High-deedy Earth whips lifegrist;
your kin-stem forfrets in checkless time.

A faith-law inholds you with frozen
return-vows to welkin-air's prime.

Fornaughted breath terrored the man
who trowed we sow continents to be:

Upcleaming limbs unfriend the bole,
but wind-quickening still is matterly.

DREGS

Sand roads through jack pines
and reindeer-lichen brains
find the thawed toe at lake edge.

Half hidden under rotten snow
that pouts as spring's smock,
the liquid lets cumulus bergs

scrape their dirty feet on its face.
Tire treads mulch muskeg recessions,
puncture the backfiring bleats

of Horizon's noise cannons.
At the boundary of solid and seep,
I raise a fibreglass pipe

to heave through deep sediment,
coring taxa from accreted sleep.
Three feet of in-situ dregs:

inwash, tills, pollen grains,
double-bunked sloughed soil
blown from pre-Agassiz mills

held in a telescope. At the lab,
luminescence interrogates
luckless seeds of interstitial trees:

ratting out uranium embedded
in its weave, the oldest dirt confesses
a glow. Dead years shine brightest

in the strata talent show,
dazzling new earth that shirks
the stalking sun and tunes out.

NOTES

The first epigraph is from the Prologue to *The Canterbury Tales* by Geoffrey Chaucer, lines 773–774. The second is taken from *The Encyclopedia of the Solid Earth Sciences* by Philip Kearey, (Wiley-Blackwell, 2009) page 354.

"Plastiglomerate": This is a term used by scientists for a type of stone comprised of sediments and other material held together by molten plastic. The poem explores a number of ancient theories regarding the formation of mountains.

"Plastiglomerate (a metamorphic translation)" is an adaptation of the preceding poem into the simplified language of Basic English (created by linguist C.K. Ogden), which contains only 850 words. The poem mimics the crystalline structure of foliated metamorphic rocks.

"Blood from a Lodestone" was created by modifying found text from William Gilbert's *On the Loadstone and Magnetic Bodies and on the Great Magnet the Earth* (translated by Paul Fleury Mottelay).

"The Canals of Mars" is dedicated to the Martian keenness of Percival Lowell. He published a monograph of the same name.

"Madstone": According to the *Encyclopedia Americana* (first published in 1829), the aforementioned stone can be "applied to the wound...till all the poison is absorbed, when it drops off. It is then soaked in warm milk or water for a time, and when removed the liquid is found to be full of a greenish-yellow scum."

"Erratics": Large stones that have been deposited by glacial action are known as erratics. A famous example is Big Rock, located outside of Okotoks, Alberta. The poem utilizes imagery from the myth of Philoctetes.

"Nicolas Steno Walks through a Door": Considered one of the founders of modern geology, Steno was famously torn between his scientific discoveries and his religious convictions. He received a shark head from Ferdinando II de' Medici in 1666.

"Roche Moutonnée, a Clipping": There is debate about the origin of the term roche moutonnée (a rock formation shaped by the passing of a glacier), with one theory contending that it was inspired by fashionable 18th century wigs that were smoothed with mutton fat, recognizable in the painting "Portrait of Mademoiselle Huquier holding a cat" by Jean-Baptiste Perronneau.

"Stone Tape Theory": One explanation for the magnitude of displaced debris that occurred during the rockslide at Turtle Mountain in 1903 (next to the town of Frank, Alberta) is a phenomenon known as acoustic fluidization. To my knowledge, the Stone Tape Theory has yet to be substantiated.

"Unsorted Till": material transported and deposited by glacial action tends to be jumbled, containing small sediments and large rocks, and can accumulate in mounds called moraines. The three "unsorted" poems are a randomized presentation of lines and text that were eroded from early drafts of this collection.

"On Marbel" is indebted to Pliny the Elder's *Natural History*. The orthographic presentation is modelled on the works of Geoffrey Chaucer.

"Karst": Researchers have noted that a prolonged period spent within a cave can result in visual and auditory hallucinations.

"Brothers" is for Ron Martin.

"Thunderstones" explores European legends about stone tools, which during the Middle Ages were not known to have been fashioned by humans. The poem is informed orthographically by Thomas Nashe's *The Vnfortvnate Traueller*.

"Unsorted Till (medial moraine)": the term K-T boundary (now more commonly known as the K-Pg boundary), refers to a visible band of rock that marks the end of the Cretaceous Period and the mass extinction event that took place at that time.

"Omphalos": Known as the "navel of the Earth," the marble monument is located in Delphi, Greece.

"Bedrock of Life" is indebted to the ideas explored by A.G. Cairns-Smith in his book *Seven Clues to the Origin of Life*, in which he posited that the process of clay crystals splitting and passing on imperfections could have been subjected to a "genetic takeover" by organic molecules, thus establishing a structure for cellular replication and evolution.

"National Academy of Science's Guided Day-Cruise of Old Earth": The Technosphere is a term given to the portion of the environment that has been utilized or inhabited by humans. Its estimated weight is thirty trillion tons.

"Pigeon Race": My thanks to the Calgary Racing Pigeon Club for teaching me about their sport and letting me spend some time with them at their clubhouse.

"Triangle Zone" is for Bap Quartero.

"Sacred Egg" is modelled orthographically on Thomas Burnet's *The Sacred Theory of the Earth*. The poem elaborates on Burnet's postulation about the origin of mountains.

"David" is a translation of Earle Birney's well-known poem of the same name into the restricted language of Basic English. The poem mimics the crystalline structure of foliated metamorphic rocks that have been subjected to extreme pressure and heat at tectonic zones of subduction.

"Kink Bands": the equation, from *Folding and Fracturing of Rocks* by John G. Ramsey, is used for calculating variation in shearing-strain increments in kink bands.

"Lithic Boat": The Gallarus Oratory is located on the Dingle Peninsula, County Kerry, Ireland.

"Rock and Stone Cold" is composed entirely from words exchanged between The Rock and "Stone Cold" Steve Austin during their encounter on an episode of *WWF Raw* that originally aired on December 25, 2009. The epigraph is taken from Robert Thorsun's book *Stone by Stone*.

"Petrified Willow Leaves" is animated by poet and philologist William Barnes and his attempts to remove elements of French, Greek, and Latin from the English language. He felt English had given up useful words for less intelligible imported ones.

"Dregs" is for Robin Woywitka and was inspired by his work in Quaternary sedimentology.

ACKNOWLEDGEMENTS

Early versions of some of these poems have appeared in the following journals, chapbooks, and anthologies: *anti.lang, Canadian Literature, Columba, Cypress Poetry Journal, filling Station, FreeFall, The Goose, GUEST,* "How Could You," (chapbook published by the Olive Reading Series of Edmonton), *The Malahat Review, Sweet Water: Poems for the Watersheds* (Caitlin Press), *talking about strawberries all of the time, Train,* and *Trouble Among the Stars.* My thanks to the editors for their support.

An early version of "Spoil-Bank Sapling" (originally titled "Slack Sapling") was shortlisted for the Vallum Poetry Prize.

"Petrified Willow Leaves" was nominated for a Pushcart prize and an Alberta Magazine Award by *FreeFall* magazine in 2022.

A selection from the manuscript was shortlisted for the Frog Hollow Chapbook Contest in 2018.

"Erratics" was scored as a piece for chamber choir by composer Amy Brandon; it was premiered by Pro Coro at the Banff Centre for the Arts on February 15, 2019.

I want to thank the following people for their advice and suggestions as I was working on the poems for this book: Nick Thran, Steven Ross Smith, Liz Howard, Nico Rogers, and Nikki Sheppy.

For technical guidance, I am very thankful to Bap Quartero and Robin Woywitka.

As well, I owe a major thanks to Adam Dickinson for his close reading and giving direction for the manuscript, and to Colin Martin for his keen-eyed editing.

I also want to thank Jenna Butler, my editor at NeWest Press, for believing in this collection. And I offer my thanks to the whole NeWest team for all the hard work they do in creating beautiful, challenging books.

Most of all, I want to thank my wife, Marsha, and my kids, Erik and Sonia, for their love and support in my creative work.

In 2017, to honour NeWest Press' 40th anniversary, we inaugurated a new poetry series to go alongside our Nunatak First Fiction, Prairie Play, and Writer as Critic series: Crow Said Poetry. Crow Said is named in honour of Robert Kroetsch's foundational 1977 novel *What The Crow Said*. The series aims to shed light on places and people outside of the literary mainstream. It is our intention that the poets featured in this series will continue Robert Kroetsch's literary tradition of innovation, interrogation, and generosity of spirit.

Tar Swan — David Martin

That Light Feeling Under Your Feet — Kayla Geitzler

Paper Caskets — Emilia Danielewska

let us not think of them as barbarians — Peter Midgley

Lullabies in the Real World — Meredith Quartermain

The Response of Weeds: A Misplacement of Black Poetry on the Prairies — Bertrand Bickersteth

Coconut — Nisha Patel

rump + flank — Carol Harvey Steski

How to Hold a Pebble — Jaspreet Singh

A NOTE ON THE TYPE

This book is typeset in Heldane, a contemporary serif designed by Kris Sowersby and published by Klim Type Foundry in 2018. It was inspired by the renaissance works of Hendrik van den Keere, Claude Garamont, Robert Granjon, and Simon de Colines. The display face is Begum, designed by Manushi Parikh and published by Indian Type Foundry in 2015.

DAVID MARTIN works as a literacy instructor in Calgary and as an organizer for the Single Onion Poetry Series. His first collection, *Tar Swan* (NeWest Press, 2018), was a finalist for the Raymond Souster Award and the City of Calgary W.O. Mitchell Book Prize. David's work has been awarded the CBC Poetry Prize, and has been shortlisted for prizes from *FreeFall*, *Vallum*, and *PRISM international*. As well, his poems have appeared in numerous journals and magazines across Canada.